The Story of
OLD GLORY

By Albert I. Mayer

Illustrated by Tom Dunnington

 CHILDRENS PRESS, CHICAGO

Library of Congress Catalog Card Number 79-110036

3 4 5 6 7 8 9 10 11 12 13 14 15 16 17 18 19 20 21 22 23 24 25 R 75 74 73

"What a glorious gift!"

Captain William Driver felt his heart swell with pride as he watched the flag streaming in the breeze. Then he turned to his wife, his mother, and the small group of friends who had come to see him off.

"How can I thank you enough?" he asked. "I have my first command. A ship of my own. And now I have a fine new flag for her."

The young captain's eyes were misty as he looked aloft again. "What a glorious sight!" he exclaimed. "What a glorious flag! Glorious is the only word. I'll call her 'Old Glory!'"

And that, at least according to the story, is how the American flag came to be called "Old Glory." Other terms of affection are the "Stars and Stripes," the "Grand Old Flag," and the "Star-Spangled Banner." But officially, it is the flag of the United States of America.

When the brig *Charles Doggett*, Captain William Driver commanding, sailed that day in 1824 there were twenty-four stars in the flag flying at her gaff. When Captain Driver retired from the sea in 1837,

there were twenty-six stars in the nation's flag. By
1922, when the Driver family presented the original
"Old Glory" to the Smithsonian Institution, the flag
of the United States of America contained forty-
eight stars. Today there are fifty stars in the flag
we hail so proudly. Created in the midst of revolution, nearly two hundred years ago, it has grown
with the nation it symbolizes.

When John Cabot discovered the North American
continent in 1497 he carried an English flag which
had the red cross of St. George on a white field.
English settlers landing at Jamestown in 1607
probably flew both this flag and the British Union
Jack. The Union Jack combined the red cross of
St. George (which represented England) with the
white cross of St. Andrew (which represented Scot-
land) on a field of blue.

6

In the years following, the British adopted still another flag, called the Red Ensign or the Red Meteor, which had a red field and the crosses of St. George and St. Andrew in a blue canton. During the colonial period, these two flags — the Union Jack and the Red Meteor — were familiar sights along the Atlantic seaboard.

On April 19, 1775, the smoldering crisis between Great Britain and her American colonies finally burst into open war. Now the Americans needed a flag of their own. George Washington chose to use what has become known as the Grand Union or Cambridge flag. This flag was the Red Meteor with six white stripes in the field of red, creating thirteen alternate red and white stripes. In this way the Americans showed that the thirteen colonies were still loyal to Great Britain, but were opposed to certain acts of king and Parliament.

On January 1, 1776, the Grand Union flag was raised at Washington's headquarters at Cambridge, Massachusetts. No one knows who designed this banner, but it was the first step in the evolution of the American flag. However, after the Declaration of Independence, on July 4, 1776, this flag no longer expressed the new nation's spirit of independence.

But when the sun rose on June 14, 1777, almost a year after the first Independence Day, there was still no national flag. On this day the session of the Continental Congress, meeting at Philadelphia's Carpenters' Hall, was being conducted by discouraged men. General Burgoyne's invasion from Canada was under way. Elsewhere the cause of those fighting for freedom seemed bleak. In the words of Thomas Paine, these were indeed "times that try men's souls."

As congressional sessions go, the one of June 14 was relatively brief. Bills were ordered paid, John Paul Jones was named commander of the *Ranger*, and a number of other maritime matters taken up.

While discussing the maritime situation, John Adams of Massachusetts stated that the Marine Committee had requested Congress to provide the navy with an official flag. The members of Congress nodded in agreement. They had seen Commodore Esek Hopkins's fleet sail from Philadelphia flying flags which had red and white horizontal stripes and a rattlesnake above the motto "Don't Tread on Me." They knew that ships of South Carolina's navy used a similar flag, but one with red and blue horizontal stripes and the motto above the rattlesnake. They also knew that ships sailing out of New England flew a flag which had a white field with the words "An Appeal to Heaven" above a green pine tree. Obviously this variety of flags was confusing and made identification of our ships difficult.

Congress therefore unanimously approved the motion: "RESOLVED, that the flag of the United States be made of thirteen stripes, alternate red and white; that the union be thirteen stars, white in a blue field, representing a new constellation."

Leaving it up to the navy to supply itself with this new flag, Congress went on to the consideration of other business. That is all there was to it! A single sentence in the *Congressional Journal* of the day.

But what an interesting situation had come about! The members of Congress had solved a maritime problem by the creation of a naval or marine flag. What they did not know was that in reality they had created a national flag.

Almost two months passed before the nation at large learned of the flag resolution. The first recorded announcement appeared on September 3 in a Philadelphia newsprint, John Dunlap's *Pennsylvania Packet And Daily Adviser*. It was not published as a story that stood on its own. There was merely a single sentence, included in a report on what the Continental Congress had done on June 14.

The flag resolution provided no specific details regarding design. It was not even specified that the stripes be horizontal. Thus the first flags were the result of the makers' whims. Some had a circle of thirteen stars, some had twelve stars with one in the center, some had a 4-5-4 arrangement, and some had a 3-2-3-2-3 arrangement.

Even the number of points on the stars varied. Although the star of heraldry has six points, most of the stars of the early flags were five-pointed. However, there were flags with six-, seven-, and even eight-pointed stars. A flag used by John Paul Jones had twelve eight-pointed stars and one star with seven points.

No one knows who designed the flag. One person who claimed this honor was Francis Hopkinson, a congressman from New Jersey, who was one of the three commissioners making up the Continental Navy Board. A poet with considerable artistic ability, Mr. Hopkinson had helped to design the seals of the State of New Jersey, the American Philosophical Society, and the College of Philadelphia. In 1780 he designed a seal for our Board of Admiralty. In a letter stating his appreciation for having his seal accepted, Mr. Hopkinson begged recognition for other "devices" he had created. Among these listed were "The Flag of the United States of America," the great seals of the United States and the Treasury Board, and work done on designing Continental currency.

For what he called his "Labours of Fancy," Mr. Hopkinson asked no payment other than a quarter cask of public wine. At a later date, however, Mr. Hopkinson submitted an itemized bill to Congress. For having designed the flag, he asked nine pounds cash or five-hundred and forty pounds in paper money. After careful consideration of the request, Congress finally stated that Mr. Hopkinson was *not the only person* who had worked on designs for the flag, and on August 3, 1781, resolved "that the report relative to the fancy-work of F. Hopkinson ought not to be acted upon."

It is only natural that over the years many legends should grow up around the flag. For example, it was long a popular belief that specific stars represented particular states. However satisfying this thought may be, it is not in keeping with historical fact.

Of all the legends, the Betsy Ross story is the most persistent — and the most charming. Her grandson, William J. Canby, first told it in 1870, almost a century after the event, while reading a paper before the Pennsylvania Historical Society.

His grandmother, Mr. Canby said, was a well-known Philadelphia seamstress whose first husband had been killed in an accident during January, 1776. This, of course, is established fact. In June, 1776, Mr. Canby went on, General George Washington, financier Robert Morris, and George Ross, an uncle of Mrs. Ross's deceased husband, paid a visit to Mrs. Ross's shop. Saying they constituted a committee appointed by Congress, the gentlemen asked Mrs. Ross to make a flag, of which they had a rough drawing.

After stating that she had never made a flag, Mrs. Ross agreed that she "would try." The stars, she said, should have five points, not six as in the sketch. Using her scissors and a piece of folded paper, she quickly demonstrated the ease with which a five-pointed star could be cut. After suggesting a number

of other minor changes accepted by the committee, she went about making what legend has it was the first flag.

Mr. Canby's paper was never published and no longer exists. While General Washington was in Philadelphia from May 22 to June 5, 1776, the Declaration of Independence had not yet been proclaimed, and until that step was taken there was no reason to replace the Union Flag with a new banner. Furthermore, there is a record of the committees appointed by the Continental Congress, their names, their functions, and their membership. No committee on the flag existed.

An authority on the history of the flag has noted that in May, 1777, Mrs. Ross was paid for making flags for Pennsylvania's navy. "It is entirely possible," he says, "that this fact led later generations of her family to claim she made the first Stars and Stripes."

Born in strife, its design uncertain, its legal status doubtful, the flag soon began forging a history and gaining an identity of its own. On February 14, 1778, at Quiberon Bay on the northwest coast of France, John Paul Jones induced the admiral of the French fleet to exchange salutes. In so doing he gained the first formal recognition of the American flag by a foreign power. Two months later Jones sailed from Brest for a raid upon the English coast. On April 24, after an hour-long battle, he defeated the British sloop *Drake*. The surrender of the *Drake* saw the "American Stars" float for the first time over a beaten foe.

As the Continental Congress thought of it, only a navy flag had been created. Washington's "ragged Continentals" still had no national banner under which to fight. Throughout the Revolution most army units went into battle carrying only their colorful state and regimental standards. In fact, more than a hundred years would pass before all units of the army would be authorized to carry the national flag. The artillery received such authorization in 1834; the infantry in 1841; and the cavalry in 1895.

The problem of supplying Washington's army with flags is illustrated by a letter which Richard Peters, Secretary of the Board of War, wrote to General Washington on May 10, 1779, almost two years after the flag resolution was passed:

> We hope to have in a short time a competent number of drums . . . as to Colours, we have refused them for another reason. The Baron Steuben mentioned when he was here that he would settle with your Excellency some plan as to Colours. It was intended that every regiment should have two Colours — one the Standard of the United States, which should be the same throughout the Army, and the other a Regimental Colour which should vary according to the facings of the Regiment. *But it is not yet settled what is the Standard of the United States.* If your Excellency will therefore favour us with your opinion on the subject we will report to Congress and request them to establish a Standard and so soon as this is done we will endeavor to get materials and order a number made sufficient for the Army . . .

Finally, on March 1, 1783, nearly a year and a half after the surrender of the British at Yorktown, Washington received a communication stating that Congress had fulfilled his request for national standards. Unhappily, delivery was never made. Lost in storage, what happened to those flags remains unknown to this day.

Although Congress did not provide the army with flags, authorities think it likely that some regiments may have carried Stars and Stripes of their own making. However, there is no historical proof. The Stars and Stripes shown in the best-known paintings of Revolutionary War scenes, as those of John Trumbull, are actually fancies on the part of the artists.

A number of Stars and Stripes said to have been carried by various regiments are still in existence. And, although Congress had not yet provided the army with flags, it is difficult to imagine that at Yorktown, where Cornwallis surrendered on October 19, 1781, there would not have been an American flag. In this case there is supporting evidence. An artistically inclined British officer painted a watercolor of Yorktown during the siege. This picture, owned by Colonial Williamsburg, Inc., shows the Stars and Stripes flying over the American fortifications.

At the conclusion of the Revolution the army was reduced to well under a thousand men. The last remaining United States warship, *Alliance*, was sold in August, 1785. From then until 1794, when our new navy was established, only American merchant ships carried the Stars and Stripes into foreign harbors. On September 30, 1787, a merchant ship, *Columbia*, under the command of Captain Robert Gray, sailed out of Boston flying the American flag. On August 10, 1790, she was back, after a 42,000-mile voyage. For the first time, the Stars and Stripes had been carried around the world.

On January 13, 1794, Congress passed a second flag resolution. Like the first, it was brief. In less than four lines it stated that, beginning on May 1, 1795, the flag should be "fifteen stripes, alternate red and white," with a union of "fifteen stars, white in a blue field." This second flag resolution was enacted as a result of the admission of Vermont (1791) and Kentucky (1792) into the Union.

By now the government was functioning under the Constitution, and legislative discussion was recorded in the *Congressional Journal.* Introduced by Stephen Bradley of Vermont, the second flag resolution met no opposition in the Senate. In the House of Representatives, however, a spirited debate followed before the resolution was passed by a vote of 50 to 42. One congressman voted against the resolution because shipowners would have to buy new flags for all their ships at a cost of sixty dollars each. It should be borne in mind that in 1794 the United States was still a small, struggling nation. There was no navy, and the bulk of the small army was far away in the Ohio Country fighting Indians. Under these circumstances many congressmen expressed the opinion that a flag resolution was too "trivial" a matter to take up their time and attention.

The most telling objection, of course, was that if stars and stripes were added with the admission of each new state, the flag would soon become cluttered.

However, the majority of congressmen were swayed by the argument that Vermont and Kentucky would be offended if they were not represented on the flag. Besides, the added stars and stripes would show foreign powers that the young nation was growing. And it was growing. Within another decade, during their expedition of 1804-1806, Lewis and Clark carried the flag across the continent to the Pacific Ocean.

The most famous American flag is the garrison standard which flew over Fort McHenry during the British bombardment on September 13-14, 1814. The sight of this flag, still flying proudly after the successful defense of the fort, inspired a twenty-two-year-old lawyer, Francis Scott Key, to write "The Star-Spangled Banner." Key's poem, set to music, soon gained immense popularity. But it was not until March 3, 1931, that a simply worded congressional bill making "The Star-Spangled Banner" the national anthem was signed by President Herbert Hoover.

The original Star-Spangled Banner was made by Mrs. Mary Pickersgill of Baltimore at a cost of $405.90. It is now on display in the United States National Museum, a bureau of the Smithsonian Institution. When this flag flew over Fort McHenry it measured 30 by 40 feet. Today, in its restored state, it measures 28 by 32 feet.

By 1817 five new states—Tennessee, Ohio, Louisiana, Indiana, and Mississippi—had been admitted into the Union. In order that they might have representation on the flag, a third flag resolution was enacted on April 4, 1818:

An Act to Establish the Flag of the United States

Sect. 1. *Be it enacted, &c.,* That from and after the fourth of July next, the flag of the United States be Thirteen horizontal stripes, alternate red and white; that the union have twenty stars, white in a blue field.

Sect. 2. *And be it further enacted,* That on the admission of every new State into the Union, one star be added to the union of the flag; and that such addition shall take effect on the fourth of July next succeeding such admission.

This resolution, re-enacted twenty-four times with the admission of a state or states into the Union, remains as the basic flag legislation. Introduced by Representative Peter H. Wendover of New York, the resolution's mention that the stripes should be horizontal marks the first congressional effort to specify details. Representative Wendover also had wished his resolution to be specific about the arrangement of the stars. Most congressmen, however, felt this should be left up to individual taste. Later in the year President Monroe stipulated that the stars should be arranged in four equal and parallel rows of five stars each.

It was not until June 12, 1912, that the relative proportions of the flag were officially determined.

On that date, President Taft issued an executive order prescribing the relative proportions of the flag and the arrangement of the stars. Later in the year he amended the order slightly. On May 29, 1916, President Wilson added another amendment.

Today's flag follows the design and proportions set in executive orders issued by President Eisenhower in 1959 and 1960. These orders fixed the position of the stars and specified that the fly (horizontal length) must be 1.9 times the hoist (vertical width). So long as these proportions are observed, a flag may be of any size. What is probably the largest flag is one displayed by the J. L. Hudson Company of Detroit. It is 235 feet long and 104 feet wide. Its stars are five and a half feet tall and the stripes eight feet wide. It weighs three quarters of a ton.

PARTS OF THE FLAG

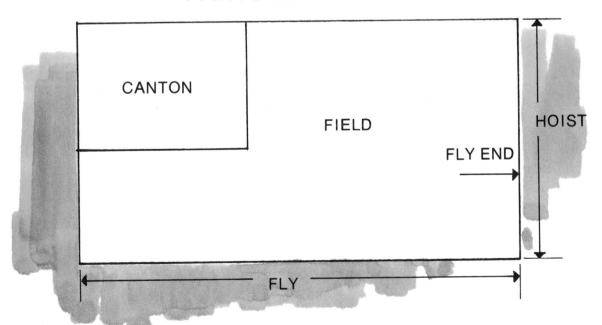

There are many customs, observances, and even laws regarding the flag. Flag Day, for example, shows how a people's love and respect for a national emblem can become a part of the law of the land.

In 1877 the government "requested" that citizens fly flags on June 14 in honor of the hundredth anniversary of the first flag resolution. Eleven years later the American Flag Day Association was founded. This organization, along with others, began urging the establishment of a national flag day. Finally, on August 3, 1949, Congress, by joint resolution, passed the National Flag Day bill designating June 14 of each year as Flag Day.

The Pledge of Allegiance is another example of a flag observance that was "adopted" by the people long before it was incorporated into law. In 1892 President Benjamin Harrison asked the schools of the nation to conduct patriotic exercises in connection with the four-hundredth anniversary of Columbus's discovery of America. The original pledge, written by Francis Bellamy was published in *The Youth's Companion*, a widely read juvenile magazine, on September 8. It was then distributed in leaflet form. On October 12, 1892, millions of schoolchildren all over the United States took the pledge.

Today the Pledge of Allegiance reads:

> I pledge allegiance to the flag of the United
> States of America and to the Republic for
> which it stands, one Nation under God,
> indivisible, with liberty and justice for all.

When first published, the pledge contained the phrase "my flag." Since this would permit a person who was born in another land to think of the flag of that country, it was felt that a change of wording was needed.

On June 14, 1923, representatives of some sixty-eight patriotic and civic organizations met in Washington, D.C. This First National Flag Conference recommended a change in the wording. The recommendation was adopted, and the words "my flag" were changed to "the flag of the United States of America." Congress made another change on June 14, 1954, by adding the words "under God."

How the flag should be displayed and honored was another matter which needed to have rules and regulations. Representatives at the First National Flag Conference wanted to draft a uniform flag code. Earlier that year the War Department had issued a circular on the rules of flag usage. This was adopted by the members of the conference.

Congress eventually assumed the task of bringing together "existing rules and customs pertaining to the display and use of the flag of the United States of America." On June 22, 1942, by joint resolution of Congress, the Code of Flag Display and Use became law.

This, then, is the story of Old Glory—a symbol of the hopes, the beliefs, and the accomplishments of a nation. As President Wilson said: "The things the flag stands for were created by the experiences of a people. Everything it stands for was written by their lives."

Albert I. Mayer, a professional writer, is the author of seven novels and over two thousand magazine articles and short stories. A former mayor of Seaside Park, N.J., his most recent novel is FOLLOW THE RIVER, dealing with the settlement of the Ohio Country during the period of the Harmar and St. Clair Campaigns, 1790-1791. Mr. Mayer recently served two terms as president of the N.J. County Library Commissioners' Association.

About the Illustrator: Tom Dunnington grew up in Iowa and Minnesota. He began his art training in Indiana and continued it at the Art Institute and the American Academy of Art in Chicago. He has five children and lives in Elmhurst, west of Chicago. Mr. Dunnington works full time as a free-lance artist. For the past three years he has taught illustration at the Layton School of Art in Milwaukee, Wisconsin.